*Greater Than a Tourist books are available in Ebook and Audiobook format.

Greater Than a Tourist Book Series

Reviews from Readers

I think the series is wonderful and beneficial for tourists to get information before visiting the city.

-Seckin Zumbul, Izmir Turkey

I am a world traveler who has read many trip guides but this one really made a difference for me. I would call it a heartfelt creation of a local guide expert instead of just a guide.

-Susy, Isla Holbox, Mexico

New to the area like me, this is a must have!

-Joe, Bloomington, USA

This is a good series that gets down to it when looking for things to do at your destination without having to read a novel for just a few ideas.

-Rachel, Monterey, USA

Good information to have to plan my trip to this destination.

-Pennie Farrell, Mexico

Great ideas for a port day.

-Mary Martin USA

Aptly titled, you won't just be a tourist after reading this book. You'll be greater than a tourist!

-Alan Warner, Grand Rapids, USA

Even though I only have three days to spend in San Miguel in an upcoming visit, I will use the author's suggestions to guide some of my time there. An easy read - with chapters named to guide me in directions I want to go.

-Robert Catapano, USA

Great insights from a local perspective! Useful information and a very good value!

-Sarah, USA

This series provides an in-depth experience through the eyes of a local. Reading these series will help you to travel the city in with confidence and it'll make your journey a unique one.

-Andrew Teoh, Ipoh, Malaysia

GREATER THAN A TOURIST- OMAHA NEBRASKA USA

50 Travel Tips from a Local

Mitzi Klimek

Cover designed by: Ivana Stamenkovic
Cover Image: https://pixabay.com/photos/omaha-nebraska-golf-course-sports-364191/

CZYK Publishing Since 2011.
Greater Than a Tourist

Lock Haven, PA

ISBN: 9798613444137

>TOURIST

50 TRAVEL TIPS FROM A LOCAL

BOOK DESCRIPTION

With travel tips and culture in our guidebooks written by a local, it is never too late to visit Omaha. Most travel books tell you how to travel like a tourist. Although there is nothing wrong with that, as part of the 'Greater Than a Tourist' series, this book will give you candid travel tips from someone who has lived at your next travel destination. This guide book will not tell you exact addresses or store hours but instead gives you knowledge that you may not find in other smaller print travel books. Experience cultural, culinary delights, and attractions with the guidance of a Local. Slow down and get to know the people with this invaluable guide. By the time you finish this book, you will be eager and prepared to discover new activities at your next travel destination.

Inside this travel guide book you will find:

Visitor information from a Local
Tour ideas and inspiration
Save time with valuable guidebook information

Greater Than a Tourist- A Travel Guidebook with 50 Travel Tips from a Local. Slow down, stay in one place, and get to know the people and culture. By the time you finish this book, you will be eager and prepared to travel to your next destination.

OUR STORY

Traveling is a passion of the Greater than a Tourist book series creator. Lisa studied abroad in college, and for their honeymoon Lisa and her husband toured Europe. During her travels to Malta, an older man tried to give her some advice based on his own experience living on the island since he was a young boy. She was not sure if she should talk to the stranger but was interested in his advice. When traveling to some places she was wary to talk to locals because she was afraid that they weren't being genuine. Through her travels, Lisa learned how much locals had to share with tourists. Lisa created the Greater Than a Tourist book series to help connect people with locals. A topic that locals are very passionate about sharing.

TABLE OF CONTENTS

BOOK DESCRIPTION
OUR STORY
TABLE OF CONTENTS
DEDICATION
ABOUT THE AUTHOR
HOW TO USE THIS BOOK
FROM THE PUBLISHER
WELCOME TO > TOURIST
1. When to Visit
2. Prepare For Every Type of Weather
3. How to Get Around
4. Omaha is Not Flat
5. Free Music
6. Free Theater
7. Free Art
8. Go Trail Running or Mountain Biking
9. Or Try One of the Paved Trails
10. Hang With a Billionaire
11. The Zoo
12. Pick a Pumpkin
13. Visit Little Italy
14. Explore Bohemia
15. Go Dancing
16. Eat some Pizza

17. Many Refugees Call Omaha Home Now
18. Join the Taco Ride
19. Visit attractions near Ashland
20. Visit Florence
21. Visit Benson
22. Eat Some Steak
23. Go Stand Up Paddle Boarding or Kayaking
24. Trains Are An Important Part of Omaha History
25. Explore Missouri River Steamboat History
26. Hang Out On A Boat
27. See Prehistoric Native American Petroglyphs
28. Trees Are Also An Important Part of Nebraska History
29. Omaha Is Centrally Located
30. Drink Some Local Brews
31. Follow Lewis and Clark
32. Visit Fort Atkinson
33. Explore Airplane History
34. Everyone Wears Red on Fall Saturdays
35. The 38th US President was Born in Omaha
36. Visit South "O"
37. Visit Dundee
38. Baseball is Big Business
39. The Olympics Are Also Big Business
40. Omaha Has Always Loved Jazz
41. Visit the Blackstone District

42. Visit Aksarben
43. The Old Market is the Heart of Omaha
44. The Locals are Nebraska Nice
45. Walk Across the Bob
46. Go On An Omaha "Homes of the Stars" Tour
47. Visit No-Do and Capitol District
48. Attend a Live Performance
49. Or Go To a Movie
50. Visit a Chapel or Cathedral with Beautiful Architecture
TOP REASONS TO BOOK THIS TRIP
Other Resources:
Packing and Planning Tips
Travel Questions
Travel Bucket List
NOTES

DEDICATION

This book is dedicated to all my friends who offered suggestions and helpful advice: Amy Brown, Dusty Zabortsky, Sharon Kazmierski, Paula Jakopovic, Melita Reineke, Doug Deden, Jerri Campbell, Dave Hedman, Mary Jo McKenna, Coleen Duda and countless others who I may have forgotten. A really big thanks to my other half, Steve Filips, for offering advice and giving me motivation to complete this book. I also dedicate this book to all those who have had the patience to travel with me and who I hope to travel with again soon.

ABOUT THE AUTHOR

Mitzi Klimek is an outdoor enthusiast who lives in Omaha, Nebraska. Mitzi loves to run, bike and participate in adventure races. Born and raised in the Sandhills of Nebraska, Mitzi moved to Omaha after college where she raised her two children, Preston & Phoebe.

Mitzi caught the travel bug when she travelled to Rome, Italy to complete her first marathon. Since then she has cruised the Mediterranean visiting Spain, France, Italy, Greece and Turkey; played on the beaches of Mexico; hiked the Inca Trail in Peru with her son; went on safari in Tanzania; toured China; and visited her homeland of England & Scotland with her sister and parents. Her goal is to visit every continent, including Antarctica and to do a race in all 50 states. Mitzi loves Omaha because all her friends are there. It seems that once you move to Omaha, you never want to live anywhere else. As a self proclaimed "foodie" and practicing Registered Dietitian, Mitzi loves the variety of ethnic cuisines in Omaha. Mitzi also loves the change in seasons. You can't appreciate 55 degrees in the spring or fall if you don't experience the 5 degrees of winter and 95 degrees of summer.

HOW TO USE THIS BOOK

The *Greater Than a Tourist* book series was written by someone who has lived in an area for over three months. The goal of this book is to help travelers either dream or experience different locations by providing opinions from a local. The author has made suggestions based on their own experiences. Please check before traveling to the area in case the suggested places are unavailable.

Travel Advisories: As a first step in planning any trip abroad, check the Travel Advisories for your intended destination.
https://travel.state.gov/content/travel/en/traveladvisories/traveladvisories.html

FROM THE PUBLISHER

Traveling can be one of the most important parts of a person's life. The anticipation and memories that you have are some of the best. As a publisher of the Greater Than a Tourist, as well as the popular *50 Things to Know* book series, we strive to help you learn about new places, spark your imagination, and inspire you. Wherever you are and whatever you do I wish you safe, fun, and inspiring travel.

Lisa Rusczyk Ed. D.
CZYK Publishing

WELCOME TO
> TOURIST

View of Downtown Omaha from Heartland of America Park

View from above West Omaha

TD Ameritrade Park Omaha

Interstate 480 leaving Omaha

"There's plenty of other places I like, but the one I love is Omaha. The weather may be a little better some other place else, but that really doesn't make much difference to me in terms of how I feel about enjoying life."

Billionaire Warren Buffett to Josh Funk at Business Insider 8/29/2012

Many people think of flat cornfields for miles when they think of Nebraska. Often referred to as a “flyover” state, many people have never experienced Nebraska and what it has to offer. They couldn’t be more wrong. In fact, Omaha and the rest of Nebraska are a best kept secret to

the locals and the few travelers who decide to check it out. From wild rivers to rolling Sandhills and some of the best stargazing and sunsets you will ever see, Nebraska is much more than the view from Interstate I-80. Some travelers love the fact that Nebraska has not been discovered, which means they don’t have to fight the crowds and have space to enjoy themselves. Nestled in the heart of farm country, Omaha has big city amenities with small town charm. The locals are friendly and enjoy low unemployment and a low cost of living. Entertainment options are plentiful with most major performers making a stop in Omaha during their tours. The arts are heavily supported with access to museums, theaters, and music venues. Omaha also has a variety of restaurants to rival any other major city. With close proximity to rural areas, you can find a place to enjoy floating on a river or running through the trees in solitude.

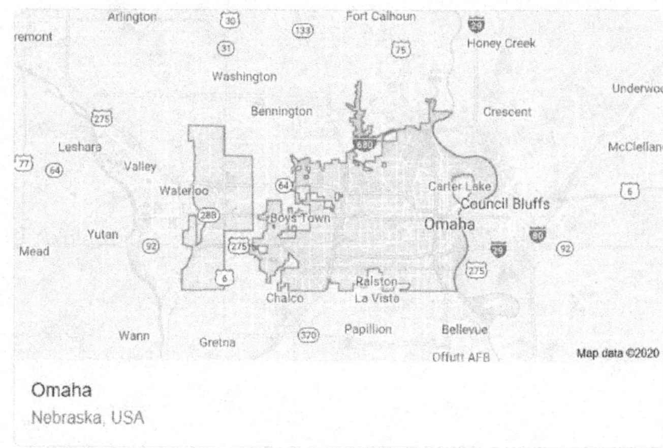
Arlington
Fort Calhoun
remont
Honey Creek
Washington
Underwoc
Bennington
Crescent
Leshara
McClellanc
Valley
Waterloo
Carter Lake
Council Bluffs
Boys Town
Omaha
Yutan
Mead
Ralston
Chalco
La Vista
Papillion
Bellevue
Wann
Gretna
Offutt AFB
Map data ©2020
Omaha
Nebraska, USA

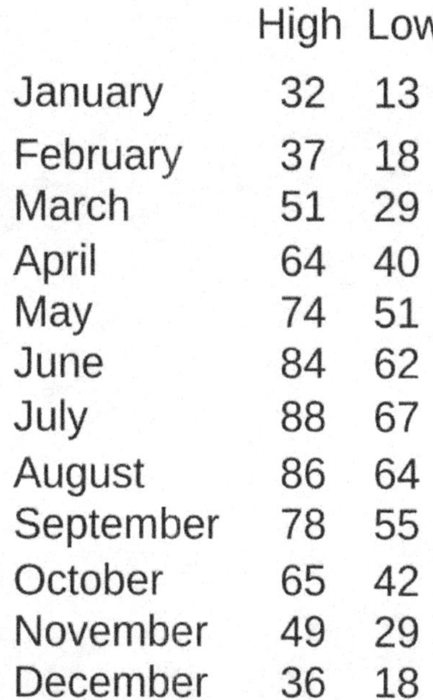

Omaha Climate

	High	Low
January	32	13
February	37	18
March	51	29
April	64	40
May	74	51
June	84	62
July	88	67
August	86	64
September	78	55
October	65	42
November	49	29
December	36	18

GreaterThanaTourist.com

Temperatures are in Fahrenheit degrees.
Source: NOAA

1. WHEN TO VISIT

The best time to visit Omaha is Spring and Fall when temperatures are mild. Unless you are a baseball fan, you may want to avoid visiting during the college world series in late June as hotels book up fast and downtown is crowded. Another busy time of year is the Berkshire Hathway Annual Shareholder meeting which is usually held the first weekend in May.

2. PREPARE FOR EVERY TYPE OF WEATHER

Nebraska is cold. Nebraska is hot. Sometimes (especially in spring and fall) Nebraska is both cold and hot on the same day. There may be a 50 degree swing in temperature in one or two days so packing layers is a must. In January or February, there may be several days below zero. In July or August, there may be several days above 100. Omaha tends to be humid during the summer but if you travel to the Sandhills in the western part of the state, the air is very dry as it is a desert.

3. HOW TO GET AROUND

Omaha is spread out with very little public transportation. Omaha does have a bus system but your best bet is to drive or use a ride share site. In the Aksarben, Midtown, and Old Market areas you can rent a bicycle or scooter to get around. Except in the Old Market area, most areas of interest are miles apart. If you are driving, pay attention to the lights on Dodge Street. Dodge street is one of the main east-west roads in Omaha and the dividing line for north & south addresses. During the morning, the center lane is for east bound traffic (towards downtown). During the evening, the center lane is for west bound traffic. Lights above the lanes denote whether you should be driving in them: red X for no driving and green O for open lanes. Left hand turns are not permitted on Dodge Street east of 72nd street. Instead you have to turn right off of Dodge to take a left. Direction on Farnam street between 57th and 42nd street also depends on the time of day as all lanes are for east bound traffic in the morning and all lanes are for west bound traffic in the afternoon. Omaha has a fairly short "rush hour". If you avoid travelling towards downtown from 7:30-8:15am or away from downtown from 4:30-5:30pm,

you will miss most of the heavy traffic. The main exception would be during college world series when traffic depends on the timing of the games.

4. OMAHA IS NOT FLAT

Nebraska is an Oto word for “flat water” and if you’ve ever driven across the state on I-80 which follows the Platter River valley you may perceive the state as flat. This is not the case. Instead, Omaha is built on rolling hills leading up from the Missouri River.

5. FREE MUSIC

During the summer, you can find free outdoor concerts on almost every day of the week. On Wednesdays, hop over the river to Bayliss Park (100 Pearl St) in Council Bluffs. Thursday has 2 very popular summer events: Jazz on the Green at Turner Park (3110 Farnam St) in the Midtown Crossing shopping area (park in the garage for free after 5pm on concert nights) and Vibes at Village Pointe (17305 Davenport St). There is a few areas to sit on the outskirts of the concerts but lawn chairs are recommended. Many people bring picnics along with wine/beer to enjoy while watching the show or purchase from vendors on site. Get there early if you want a spot close to the band as both venues fill up early. Friday night's Bridge Beats on the Nebraska side of the Bob Kerrey pedestrian bridge is my favorite outdoor concert venue. It attracts the same bands as the other venues but the crowd tends to be a lot smaller. Again you can bring your own food/beer/wine and chairs but there is also seating right next to the dance floor and the ground has enough slope that you can see the band well while sitting on a blanket. The Lewis & Clark National Historic Trail Visitor's Center (601 Riverfront Dr) is next door and stays open until 8pm on concert nights and provides free parking for the show. Rockbrook Village at 108Th and Center and Shadow Lake Shopping Center at 72nd St and Hwy 370 in Papillion also host concerts on Friday nights during the summer. On Saturday nights, Stinson Park (2232 S 64th) hosts Saturdays @ Stinson at Aksarben Village. This is also a very popular venue but it is large enough that you can get a good spot even if you arrive later. You will want to bring your own chairs and may bring your own food/drinks or there are vendors available to purchase food and beverages. Inside the park there is also a playground and splash fountain to keep the kids busy.

6. FREE THEATER

June & July are the months for free Shakespeare in Omaha. For three weekends (Thursday-Sunday), actors from across the US take the stage to perform two plays at the annual Shakespeare on the Green. The plays take place in Elmwood Park next to the University of Nebraska Omaha campus. For the best viewing, go in the morning and throw down a blanket to mark your spot. There is an area marked for low chair/blanket seating. Otherwise you can bring lawn chairs and sit in the chair section. Food trucks are on site or you may bring your own picnic/beverages. I like to get there early to people watch and listen to the wandering minstrels who perform before the play. This is a free event fully funded by donations so be generous if you can!

7. FREE ART

Near the TD Ameritrade Baseball Stadium and Creighton University lies the Hot Shops Art Center (1301 Nicholas Street). Eighty plus artists create their art in their own personal galleries. Hot Shops hosts 2 open houses each year which are very popular (aka crowded) events. Instead I prefer to go during the week when I can peruse the art and talk to the local artists at my leisure. On a recent trip with my 2 nieces (ages 5 & 7), they were able to blow glass in the glass studio, watch a potter create a bowl, walk into her kiln that is large enough for several adults, and observe painters and jewelry makers. If you are more interested in classic art, then I would recommend the Joslyn Art Museum. This museum located at 2200 Dodge St is also free to the public. There are 2 entrances on the East side of the building with free parking on the north side of the building. I prefer to enter through the southernmost entrance at the top of the Grand Staircase. This entrance is closest to the Renaissance & Impressionist Art. If you are traveling with children, stop by the Scott EdTech Gallery first where they can get scavenger hunts and Art Packs to help them explore the museum. Also be sure and stop by the Art Works area in the basement where they can play and create their own art. For modern art, head over to Kaneko. Located at 1111 Jones Street on the south side of the Old Market, Kaneko was started by international artist Jun Kaneko and his wife. In addition to rotating art exhibits, Kaneko also hosts performances, lectures and creative educational workshops. Local budding artists showcase their art at Amplify Art's Generator Space at 1804 Vinton Street. This nonprofit provides grant money to support developing artists along with a larger platform for them to exhibit their art. It is free and open to the public on Thursday & Friday afternoons.

8. GO TRAIL RUNNING OR MOUNTAIN BIKING

Omaha has a very committed group of volunteers who maintain single track trails at various locations around the Omaha metro area. If you google "Trails Have Our Respect", aka THOR, you will find information about all the trails that they maintain. My favorite trails for biking and running are Swanson just east of 36th & Cornhusker in Bellevue and

Tranquility west of 120th St between Maple and Fort St. The entrance to Swanson can be tricky to find as it is not marked on Cornhusker Street. To find Swanson, take Cornhusker Road west from Hwy 75 until you see a sign for the Bellevue fire department. Turn right at that sign and follow the road down into the parking lot and playground area. You will see the trail head near the entrance of the parking lot. There is a sign at the trail head that says "Bikes Only" but runners and hikers are also welcome to use the trail. Tranquility Park can be accessed from either Maple Street or Fort Street. From Maple Street, turn north on 124th St and follow the signs to the Tim Moylan Tranquility IcePlex. The trail head is marked by a kiosk near the top parking lot. From Fort St, take your first left west of 120th St into the park and drive past the soccer fields to the trail head. The Fort Street trailhead will take you into the trees right away while the Maple Street trailhead is more exposed to sun and wind near the top of a hill. All of the THOR trails are in low crime areas but you should be aware that thieves have been known to target the cars of runners/cyclists. It is highly recommended that you leave nothing in sight in your car while enjoying the trails. The local trail running group is called the GOATZ, not to be confused with the Omaha Rugby team which is also the Goats. If you are looking for someone to show you around a local trail, a quick post to their Facebook page (Greater Omaha Area Trail Runners) will usually result in several volunteers.

9. OR TRY ONE OF THE PAVED TRAILS

There are 120 miles of paved bike paths in Omaha. The City of Omaha Parks and Recreation Department has maps of all the trails. You can get a copy of the map titled "Paths of Discovery" by visiting their website or pick up one at the libraries or local bike shop. My favorite paved trail for running is the 5.5-mile loop around Wehrspann Lake. The paths around Lake Zorinsky are also very popular. 168th Street crosses over the lake, dividing the paths in half. The east half is a 4.5-mile loop, the west side is a 3-mile loop. If you are looking for group runs, check out the Run 402 Facebook page.

10. HANG WITH A BILLIONAIRE

Warren Buffet is one of the richest people in the world. The home that he bought in 1958 is still his current residence and you can stroll down the street by it on the southwest corner of 55th & Farnam. Pop into the nearby McDonalds at breakfast time or Gorat's Steakhouse for dinner and you may end up eating near him. Stop in to Dairy Queen for a snack in the middle of the afternoon for another chance to see him. For the best chance to see him, buy one share of stock in his Berkshire Hathway Inc and attend the annual shareholders meeting that is held in May in Omaha each year. Over 30,000 people descend on Omaha for the weekend which has been called "the Woodstock of Capitalism".

11. THE ZOO

Ranked as the #1 zoo in the world by TripAdvisor, no trip to Omaha is complete without a visit to the Henry Doorly Zoo. The large "Desert Dome" can be seen from I-80 near the 13th Street exit. This is a very popular place to be during the summer and traffic often will back up onto I-80. To skip the line of cars, approach the zoo from the north on 10th street. This will put you closer to the less popular North entrance to the zoo. During the winter, go ahead and use the 13th Street entrance as the zoo's north entrance is usually closed. My 2 favorite attractions at the zoo are the Scott Aquarium and the Kingdom of the Night exhibit in the basement of the Desert Dome. My daughter loves the Butterfly Pavilion and the Orangutan building. If you are visiting during the summer with kids, bring swimsuits or a change of dry clothes so they can play in the water feature in the Children's Adventure Trails area. You can bring your own food and drinks into the zoo or for a change of pace you can try the African cuisine while watching elephants at the African Lodge.

12. PICK A PUMPKIN

If you are visiting in September or October, I'd suggest a trip to Vala's Pumpkin Patch (12102 S 180th St, Gretna). With 50+ attractions on 400 acres, it is more amusement park than pumpkin patch. I'd recommend going during the week if possible. To avoid the traffic lines on the weekends, take I-80 to the Gretna exit, head north to Schram Road and then head east on Schram to the pumpkin patch. On a recent weekend trip, I made the mistake of taking Hwy 370 to 180th Street and then south to the pumpkin patch. We sat in traffic for over an hour to move 1.5 miles. A lower cost, less crowded venue with plenty to do is the Skinny Bones Pumpkin Patch. It is located north of Omaha on Hwy 133 on the way to Blair, Nebraska. Skinny Bones also hosts a free will donation gravel run (the Goatz Gravel Classic) every May where runners can enjoy 30k or 60k of rolling gravel hills while supporting local charities.

13. VISIT LITTLE ITALY

A few minutes south of downtown Omaha is the Little Italy neighborhood. Originally settled by Sicilian immigrants, now it is home to a mix of cultures. To sample some of the classic Italian food, I'd recommend lunch from the Ethnic Sandwich Shop at 1438 S 13th Street. Frequented by local tradesmen, the shop is only open on week days and has no indoor seating. If you are searching for old Italian pizza, try Orsi's Italian Bakery and Pizzeria at 621 Pacific Street. The pizzeria originated with the Sicilian immigrants and has been in operation for 100 years. With limited seating, I'd recommend calling in your order and taking it to go.

14. EXPLORE BOHEMIA

A "new" old area of Omaha within Little Italy is Little Bohemia. The much beloved Bohemian Café was located on 13th Street but unfortunately closed several years ago. Local entrepreneurs are trying to resurrect the Bohemian influence in the area. The Infusion Bar located within the old Bohemian Café is trying to keep the feel alive by hosting Polka Pot Lucks on the first Sunday of the month with polka music, just bring a Bohemian dish to share. If you love polka music, you can also visit the German American Society located in western Omaha off of 120th street between Center & I Street.

Amongst Little Italy and Little Bohemia is Olsen Bake Shop. Started in 1942, this bake shop at 1708 S 10th Street often has customers lined up out the door.

Not much has changed inside the shop since it opened including the love that goes into their donuts, cookies and kolaches. These are goodies that feel like your grandma just pulled them out of the oven.

15. GO DANCING

You can find cover bands playing at various bars all over the city. The Ozone, attached to Anthony's Steakhouse on 72nd street just south of I-80, is a very popular dance spot for the 40+ crowd. Another popular dance spot is Two Fine Irishmen in west Omaha near 180th & Q. There is no cover charge and the dance floors are always packed at both locations. For DJ music with an eclectic crowd of all ages, head to The Max at 1417 Jackson Street. Put the address in your phone, there is no sign outside so it is easy to miss.

16. EAT SOME PIZZA

If you want to start a debate, ask someone where the best pizza is in Omaha. We have numerous pizza places and each one is a someone's favorite, therefore I am only going to talk about three of them. The first pizza place that I would recommend is Via Farina at 1108 S 10th Street. You can walk there from downtown or there is free street parking nearby. It is not your classic Neopolitan Pizza. I love it because I can sit at the back counter to eat and watch them make their handmade brickoven pizzas and pastas. I call it "dinner with a show". The second pizza place that I would recommend is Lighthouse Pizza located at 1004 S 74th Plaza and 1170 Capitol Avenue. You order by the slice at the counter and you get to pick 5 toppings per slice. The slices are huge so I usually share 1 slice with a friend. You can also order super fries which are fries loaded with toppings such as brisket, pulled pork, blue cheese, etc. The third pizza shop on my list is Tasty Pizza at 5423 Leavenworth Street. Located inside a house, they prepare individual size pizzas from fresh ingredients. The parking lot and dining room are both rather small so I usually get my order to go.

17. MANY REFUGEES CALL OMAHA HOME NOW

Sudan, Somalia, & Nepal are just a few of the countries that were once home to our refugees. You can see their influence in different areas of Omaha. I like to explore their heritage through their food. Three of my favorite restaurants are Mai Thai near 68th & Center, Lalibela Ethiopian on Saddlecreek, and Jaipur Indian near 108th & Center. Another option is to eat at the International Café at 2416 Farnam Street. The décor is worn down but the food is good and you can watch Al Jazeera on TV while you eat.

18. JOIN THE TACO RIDE

Every Thursday night, hundreds of cyclists show up to the Wabash Trail head in Council Bluffs near Lewis Central School to ride to Toby Jacks's Steakhouse in Mineola and eat tacos. There is no set start time as people join in whenever they can get there. About half way to Mineola is a picnic area called "Margaritaville" where many riders stop to take a break, visit with other cyclists and enjoy beverages that they have brought along. Helmets are recommended as the trail is crowded and wrecks do happen on occasion, especially on the ride back to Council Bluffs after some people enjoy alcoholic beverages with their tacos. Bike lights or flashlights attached to your bike are also recommended as there is no light along the trail and unless you get there early, it will probably be dark for your ride home.

19. VISIT ATTRACTIONS NEAR ASHLAND

Clustered together about 20 minutes west of Omaha on I-80 are 3 popular attractions: Strategic Air Command & Aerospace Museum, The Lee G Simmons Wildlife Safari Park, and Mahoney State Park. For a nice day trip, I'd recommend checking out the 300,000 square feet Aerospace Museum in the morning. Take a picnic or drive north into the town of Ashland for lunch. Burn off your lunch by swimming, rock climbing, hiking or playing on the ropes course at Mahoney State Park. End your day with a drive through the Lee G Simmons Conservation Park & Wildlife Safari where you can see Elk & Buffalo roaming the park. Make sure and get out of your car and hike up to see the Wolves, black bears, eagles, and whooping cranes.

20. VISIT FLORENCE

Founded in 1854, this village in the north east corner of Omaha has many historic sites to visit. To get there, take hwy 75 north out of downtown and then stay north on 30th street. Or you can get there by getting off of I-680 and heading south at the 30th street exit. In 1846-1847, Florence was the Winter Quarters for 2,500 Mormon migrants. You can learn about their history by visiting the Mormon Trail Center at 3215 State Street. The only surviving building that was built by the Mormons is Florence Mill (or Weber Mill) nearby at 9102 N 30th. It now contains a museum, art gallery and hosts a Farmer's Market during the summer. No trip to Florence would be complete without a visit to Harold's Koffee House at 8327 N 30th for some coffee, donuts, old fashioned cooking and atmosphere.

21. VISIT BENSON

Best visited in the evening, the Benson neighborhood is located on Maple Street between 60th & 63rd Streets. Refurbished in recent years, it has a variety of bars, restaurants and breweries. One of my favorite, quick lunch spots is Star Deli tucked on the northeast side of the Maple & Military intersection. For lunch or dinner, I'd recommend the Benson Brewery especially if it is a nice night to sit out on the deck. The star attraction in Benson is The Waiting Room, an indie rock club that brings in talent from all over the country.

22. EAT SOME STEAK

Omaha is in the heart of cattle country. Steak is so important here that we only have 2 stores in our airport. One sells magazines, snacks and other travel related needs. The other store sells steak. I would say that the best steak in Omaha is one that was raised on my parent's ranch in western Nebraska and cooked in my own kitchen. Unfortunately, that is not an option for most. The Drover at 2121 S 73rd Street was by far the number 1 pick when I polled my Facebook friends. Flemings at 140 Regency Parkway and Jericho at 11732 West Dodge were distant 2nd and 3rd picks.

23. GO STAND UP PADDLE BOARDING OR KAYAKING

Several small "no wake" lakes dot the west side of Omaha and provide tranquil water for Stand Up Paddle Boarding. My 3 favorite spots are Wehrspann Lake in south west Omaha, Standing Bear Lake in north west Omaha, and Walnut Creek Lake south of Omaha. All three lakes have boat docks for easy entry onto the lake as well as paved bike trails around the lake. If you don't have your own board, you can rent one from Driftwood Paddle Board Adventures, the UNO Venture Center, or Play It Again Sports near 84th & Center. If you prefer rivers, the Platte River has convenient entry and exit points for kayaking near Omaha. I'd recommend getting on the river at the Platte River State Access site located on Hwy 64 west of Valley, Nebraska. From there you can kayak down to the take out at Two Rivers State Recreation Area.

There is a $5 day use fee at Two Rivers which also has camping and shower facilities. This float will take about 3-5 hours, the drive back to Hwy 64 is only 10-15 minutes. WoggWorks Kayaking offers kayak rental and guided river trips. During the winter, they offer kayak lessons at in indoor pool. Tubing and Adventures in Waterloo, Nebraska also offers kayak trips and tubing trips. For more local advice on kayaking, canoeing or SUPing, visit the Nebraska Canoe and Kayak Facebook page.

24. TRAINS ARE AN IMPORTANT PART OF OMAHA HISTORY

The First Transcontinental railroad started in Omaha in 1863. Union Pacific continues to have its headquarters in Omaha. If you are a train fanatic, there are 3 locations that you should check out. First, visit Kenefick Park to see "Big Boy", the world's largest steam engine locomotive. The path leading up to big boy and Kenefick Park is located just south of the Lauritzen Garden parking lot. From the park you can also get a nice view of the Missouri River and Interstate I80. The second location is sout on 10th street, the Durham Museum. This Smithsonian Museum is housed within Union Station, an old train depot. It has a multitude of permanent and traveling exhibits along with an old passenger train that you can walk through and see what it would have been like to ride the rails years ago. The third location is the Union Pacific Railroad Museum located across the river in Council Bluffs. If you only have time for 1 train museum, my favorite is the Union Pacific Railroad Museum. The museum is free on the night of the first Friday of the month.

25. EXPLORE MISSOURI RIVER STEAMBOAT HISTORY

In 1865, Steamboat Bertrand sank on the Missouri River about 30 miles north of Omaha. It was entombed in mud until it was discovered in 1968 and excavated. The artifacts (about 250,000) that were preserved in the mud are on display in the Visitor Center of the DeSoto National Wildlife Center near the location where it originally sank.

26. HANG OUT ON A BOAT

The River City Star offers day and evening cruises on the Missouri River. It docks at the Dam Bar and Grill at 151 Freedom Park Road. Also located nearby is the Freedom Park Navy Museum where you can see the USS Marlin SST-2 Submarine and the USS Hazard AM-240 Minesweeper. Unfortunately, Freedom Park sits very close to the river and is frequently closed due to flooding so it's best to check the Omaha Parks and Recreation website to see if it is open.

The River Inn Resort south of Omaha in Brownville, Nebraska offers the opportunity to sleep on a boat on the Missouri River. You can also book a dinner cruise on The Spirit of Brownville. While in Brownville, you can visit historic museums and shop in local boutiques and galleries. If you want to stay on land and watch boats go by, I'd suggest hanging out at Surfside at 14445 North River Drive north of Omaha. It has a limited food and drink menu but on a summer day it is relaxing place to hang out and observe boaters and water skiers. They also have an outdoor stage where local cover bands play in the evening.

27. SEE PREHISTORIC NATIVE AMERICAN PETROGLYPHS

A few minutes south of Brownville is Indian Cave State Park. There you can see a cave where prehistoric Americans left their mark. The Park also offers Living History weekends where you can learn how to make soap or candles or blacksmith items. There is also a restored 1 room schoolhouse and general store to explore. This park also has great trails for hiking and mountain biking. The Steamboat Trace trail is a limestone packed trail for hiking and biking that connects Brownville to Nebraska City. A local man, Roland Sherman, created many carvings in the sandstone cliffs along the trail between Brownville and Peru. He started his carvings back when trains still ran along the cliffs instead of bicycles. His son says he carved them with a pocket knife to entertain himself and his grandkids.

28. TREES ARE ALSO AN IMPORTANT PART OF NEBRASKA HISTORY

Arbor Day got its start in Nebraska City in 1872 when 1 million trees were planted. Today you can visit the home of Arbor Day at Arbor Day Farm. There are tree related activities for the kids and wine tastings for the parents. It is a very popular location in the fall when the apples are ripe and ready to be picked. The home of Arbor Day founder, J. Sterling Morton, has been preserved and is open to the public at the Arbor Lodge State Historical Park and Arboretum. This fifty-two-room mansion contains historic artifacts and authentic furnishings. The surrounding 65 acres contain 260 species of trees and shrubs. Some of the older trees were planted by Morton himself. The grounds are free and open year-round, there is a small fee to enter the mansion which is only open on the weekends during the winter and daily during the summer. If you head 2 hours north of Omaha to Ponca State Park, you can see one of the oldest trees in the state. Dubbed "the Old Oak Tree", it began life in 1644 making it 143 years older than the US Constitution and 223 years older than the

State of Nebraska. Besides the Oak Tree, Ponca also has 22 miles of mountain bike & hiking trails. Within the park is a tri-state overlook where one can see South Dakota, Nebraska & Iowa dissected by the Missouri River.

29. OMAHA IS CENTRALLY LOCATED

Omaha is half way between Chicago & Denver, 8 hours from each. It is slightly closer to Canada (9 hours to Winnepeg) than it is the Gulf of Mexico (13 hours to Houston). Whichever direction you may be headed, I recommend you spend a few days and enjoy the heartland.

When Omaha hosted the 1898 World's Fair, it was dubbed the "Gateway to the West" due to its location and importance as a transportation hub. Steamboats traveled along the Missouri River hauling goods and people. Railroads through Omaha connected the east and west coasts. Settlers in covered wagon caravans stopped in Omaha to stock up with supplies as they continued traveling west. Today, along with the railroads, Interstate I-80 through Omaha continues to be an important eastwest route across the US.

30. DRINK SOME LOCAL BREWS

Every day, there seems to be a new brewery opening up in Omaha. Brickway Brewer and Distillery in the Old Market at 1116 Jackson Street offers tours, food and my favorite coffee vanilla stout. My fiance prefers their Honest American Single Malt Whisky or Hef beer. Vis Major Brewing at 3501 Center Street offers trivia on Monday nights and board games every day along with their excellent brews. Try their Eden Shade Apricot Ale or 22 Bones Dark Coconut Wheat. Scriptown Brewery located at 3922 Farnam Street in the Blackstone district serves Kathmandu Momos through a hole in the wall between them and the Nepalese Street Food restaurant located next door. They also host a running club on Thursday nights. Try their Nutjob Brown Ale or an Ups & Downs blend of beer with coffee. The Omaha Visitors Center ,306 S. 10th Street, offers a free souvenir flight glass as well as Omaha's Craft Brew Penny Pack which gives you a "buy one get one for a penny" coupons to 12 local breweries. The Penny Pack is available on the visit Omaha website. If you are looking for a one stop place to try several different regional beers, there a couple bars in town to try. The Casual Pint, located at 8718 Countryside Plaza within Countryside Village, has 28 rotating craft beers on tap, many of which are regional to Nebraska. In addition to the tap beers, they have 2 walls of mix and match canned and bottled beers for purchase to drink there or to take home. The Local Beer, Patio & Kitchen at 4909 S 135th Street also has a rotating selection of local beers on tap. Sometimes you just want to find a local "hole in the wall" bar and relax. The Trap Room at 733 N 14th Street isn't easy to spot as it is tucked back behind Hook and Lime. With dark décor and a 70s basement vibe, the bartenders serve an impressive array of beer and cocktails. My friends insist that the Homy Inn at 1510 N Saddlecreek must also be mentioned. Don't let the Champagne on Tap confuse you and make you think it's a fancy place. The Homy Inn is definitely a "dive bar" with nostalgic newspapers, restaurant menus and an homage to Elvis Presley on the walls. Heading south to Ralston, dive into the Village Bar at 5700 S 77th Bar. This local dive is usually packed on the weekends and offers classic entertainment such as dart boards, skee-ball, and live music.

31. FOLLOW LEWIS AND CLARK

Between 1803 and 1806, the Lewis and Clark expedition traveled from Pennsylvania across the westward portion of America to the Pacific Ocean. Their voyage by boat up the Missouri River to map and explore the newly purchased territories passed through what is now modern-day Omaha, NE and Council Bluffs, IA. The only casualty of the journey was Sergeant Charles Floyd, a monument overlooking the river marks his burial site approximately 90 miles north of Omaha on interstate I-29. To learn more about their local stay, and journey, visit the Lewis and Clark National Historic Trail Headquarters and Visitors center at 601 Riverfront Dr. An equally impressive exhibit is on display at the Western Historic Trails Center, just across their river at 3434 Richard Downing Ave in Council Bluffs. Both visitor centers have immediate access to a large network of trails along the Missouri River. For a great panoramic view of Omaha, travel to the Lewis and Clark Monument Park at 19962

Monument Rd just north of Council Bluffs. This park is also a great place to hike and mountain bike. The entrance to the trails is near the park entrance off of Monument Road. Beware- the trail starts and finishes at the highest point and drops quickly in elevation; save some energy for the climb back up.

32. VISIT FORT ATKINSON

Fort Atkinson was established in 1820 and was the first U.S. Military Post west of the Missouri River. It operated from 1820 and 1827 and during that time, 1200 U.S. soldiers lived there (almost 1/4th of the Standing US Army at the time). The fort has been reconstructed and living history exhibits take place throughout the summer. To visit, take hwy 75 north out of Omaha to the town of Fort Calhoun. Fort Atkinson is on the east side of town.

33. EXPLORE AIRPLANE HISTORY

Home to the Offutt Airforce Base, airplanes have played a role in Omaha's history since 1910 when a Wright Brother's plane was flown at the Nebraska State Fair. In the 1940s, the local Martin Bomber Plant produced Boeing B-29 Superfortresses. The two most notable planes produced there were the Enola Gay and Bockscar which dropped the atomic bombs on Hiroshima and Nagasaki. Today, you can see a variety of military planes and spacecraft on display at the Strategic Air Command and Aerospace Museum near Ashland, Nebraska.

34. EVERYONE WEARS RED ON FALL SATURDAYS

Nebraskans love the Huskers! This may seem like a generalization and there are some Nebraskans who say they do not like cornhusker football but on game day Saturdays, red is everywhere. This is even more true in Lincoln, the home of the Huskers when Memorial Stadium (with 92,000 seats) becomes the third largest city in the state. Another interesting phenomenon is that stores and area attractions are empty while the Huskers are playing. If you happen to be traveling between Omaha and Lincoln on home game Saturdays, be prepared for backups on I-80 and Hwy 6. While the football team gets most of the attention, the Husker volleyball team is almost always ranked in the top 10 in the country.

35. THE 38TH US PRESIDENT WAS BORN IN OMAHA

Gerald R Ford was born in Omaha on July 14, 1930. Originally named Leslie Lynch King, Jr, he lived in Omaha in his grandparents home for a very short time. The location of the home at 3202 Woolworth Ave contains a memorial to the president along with a rose garden modeled after the rose garden at the White House.

36. VISIT SOUTH "O"

The Hispanic heart of Omaha stretches south from the intersection of L St. and south 24th St. Home of the annual Cinco de Mayo street festival, the streets are lined with Hispanic shops, markets, taquerias and restaurants. Down the main drag, just past most of the shops, is Taqueria El Rey with a good-sized selection of authentic Mexican dishes. Or look for their food truck at different locations around town. Turn the corner off of 24th street for a short walk to El Museo Latino, a small museum showcasing Latino arts and culture of the Americas.

37. VISIT DUNDEE

Start your visit of the Dundee neighborhood at the intersection of north 50th St. and Underwood Ave. Walk west for dinner from a coal fired oven at Pitch Pizzeria. Work your way back east and look for the plaque marking the location where a Japanese balloon bomb exploded over Dundee in April 1945. Luckily, there was no casualties. Stop in for a nightcap at the Dundee Dell and try a sample or two from their Wall of Scotch that has over 700 bottles to choose from. Or try gelato or ice cream at eCreamery and take advantage of their shipping to send ice cream pints to someone you love.

38. BASEBALL IS BIG BUSINESS

No, Omaha does not have a pro baseball team but once a year it becomes a college baseball mecca. In mid June the College World Series comes to town and TD Ameritrade Park just north of downtown is the place to be if you love baseball. If you are thinking about coming to Omaha for the World Series, book your hotel or AirBNB early! If you are not interested in baseball and don't want to fight the crowds, I'd recommend checking the dates of the College World Series and planning your trip for a different time.

39. THE OLYMPICS ARE ALSO BIG BUSINESS

You are probably wondering what Omaha has to do with the Olympics. Well, the lack of pro sports in Omaha has made locals get excited for any type of sport that comes to town. And right now, those 2 sports are Swimming & Curling. Omaha has been lucky enough to be chosen by the US Olympic Swim Trials for several years. The US Olympic Curling Trials have also chosen Omaha as their host city twice in a row. The entire city supports these events and downtown Omaha gets a makeover with swim themed activities and murals when the trials are in town.

40. OMAHA HAS ALWAYS LOVED JAZZ

Through the 1920s to 1960s, Omaha was a frequent stop for top Jazz musicians such as Nat King Cole, Dizzy Gillespie, and Louis Armstrong. Today you can enjoy jazz at the Jewell in the Capital District north of downtown. You can learn about Omaha jazz and African American history at Love's Jazz and Art Center (2510 N 24th St), named after local jazz legend, Preston Love.

41. VISIT THE BLACKSTONE DISTRICT

Named after the Blackstone Hotel at 36th and Farnam, this area is newly revitalized and home to unique bars and restaurants. The nearby Crescent Moon still serves the original Blackstone Rueben that was created by Rueben Kulakofsky at his weekly poker game within the Blackstone Hotel. Located in the basement of the Crescent Moon is the Huber Haus German Bier Hall where you can drink Das Boot (a glass boot filled with 2 liters of beer and specific game rules) with your friends. If tequila is more your style, head down to Mula for a sip along with authentic Mexican street food. Free parking is available in any of the UNMC lots after 4pm on weekdays and all day on the weekends.

42. VISIT AKSARBEN

The Aksarben area (Nebraska spelled backwards) started off as a horse racetrack and nearby airfield in the 1920's. Look for the two historical markers on 67th St., north of West Center St.; one to mark the historical importance to air mail delivery and the second marking the burial site of the racehorse Omaha, the 1935 Triple Crown winner. More recently, it was redeveloped into a restaurant, shopping and cinema district with Stinson Park on the southern end. Bring lawn chairs and snacks/drinks for live music in the park on weekends or visit the Farmer's Market held here on Sunday mornings May-October. Check out the large variety of menu options available at Beacon Hill or the very authentic cajun and creole flavors at Herbe Sainte. If you are with a large party and need multiple options, try the Inner Rail Food Hall. It is a modern-day food court with vendors from local restaurants instead of the classic fast food chains.

43. THE OLD MARKET IS THE HEART OF OMAHA

If you only have 1 day in Omaha, spend most of your time visiting the Old Market in downtown Omaha. Unlike some cities where the downtown business district empties at night, Omahans flock to the downtown area for great restaurants, plays, symphonies, museums, boutique shopping, and art galleries. Downtown has a farmer's market on Saturday mornings May-October. The Orpheum and Holland Performing Arts Center are located nearby along with the Heartland of America Park. There is plenty of meter and garage parking. If you are not averse to walking, you can park for free at the top of the 10th street bridge on the south side of downtown. The parking garage at the base of the 10th street bridge has the cheapest rate of all the garage parking in the downtown area. My three favorite restaurants in the Old Market are Ahmad's Persian Food, Shahi Indian, and Plank fresh seafood. Be sure and step inside the picturesque Passageway between 10th & 11th street on the north side of Howard.

44. THE LOCALS ARE NEBRASKA NICE

The Urban Dictionary defines Nebraska Nice as when a person is genuinely polite and courteous without having a hidden agenda. This is true for most locals that you will encounter on your visit. Omahans will try to be helpful, offer advice, and give directions. If you get off I-80 in the western part of the state, the locals will wave by raising their index finger off the steering wheel as they meet you on the highway. It's a reflex that they learn in childhood along with offering assistance to someone in need.

45. WALK ACROSS THE BOB

The Bob Kerry foot bridge stretches over the Missouri River, connecting Omaha to Council Bluffs, Iowa. The "Bob" connects Omaha trails to a network of trails in Iowa that extend north and south. Bike rental stations are available on both sides of the river. The bridge and trails are a popular walking destination that at 3000 feet high provide great views of the skyline year-round. Near the high point of the bridge, the border line is etched and makes it possible to get a picture standing in Iowa and Nebraska at the same time.

46. GO ON AN OMAHA "HOMES OF THE STARS" TOUR

Several Oscar nominated Stars were born and raised in Omaha. You can still drive by and see where some of them lived. Silent film star Harold Lloyd moved to Omaha from his home in Burchard, Nebraska as a teenager and lived in a hotel that was located where the current Omaha World Herald building sits. Fred Astaire lived at 2326 S 10th Street until he was 6 years old. Montgomery Clift lived at 2101 S 3rd Street. As a baby, Marlon Brando lived at 3135 Mason Street until his family moved to a bigger house nearby at 1026 S. 32nd Street. An apartment building now stands were Dorothy McGuire lived at 602 S 38th Ave. Henry Fonda grew up in the house at 5108 California Street and got his start in acting at the Omaha Community Playhouse which was then located at 4016 Farnam Street. Henry's children, Jane and Peter Fonda, spent summers in Omaha at their aunt's home at 5205 Izard Street and both also acted at the Omaha Community Playhouse. Nick Nolte lived at 2301 N 56th Street and played football for Benson Highschool. His senior year he moved to a house at 1150 S. 94th Street and graduated from Westside Highschool. Alexander Payne graduated from Creighton Prep Highschool and his family's restaurant was located where the W. Dale Clark Library now sits. Another famous Omaha native is Malcolm X. El Hajj Malik el Shabazz (aka Malcolm X) was born and named Malcolm Little in 1925 at his parent's home located at 3448 Pinkney Street. Unfortunately, the original home was demolished in the 1960s. The Malcolm X Memorial

Foundation now owns the 15 acres surrounding the home. The site contains a historical marker and visitor center. The center is staffed by volunteers so the hours may vary. Your best bet is to call ahead to make sure the center is open. The historical marker is located behind the visitor center.

47. VISIT NO-DO AND CAPITOL DISTRICT

Several blocks north of the Old Market, the new Capitol District merges with the north-downtown (No-Do) area. By far, the biggest draw in the area is the 18,000 seat CHI Health Center arena and convention center. Home to numerous sporting events, concerts and conventions, the CHI Health Center has hosted most major-name touring entertainers, NCAA Men's Basketball Tournament games and is the home of Creighton University Men's Basketball team. Look for a sea of Creighton blue shirts and sweaters when the local bars, restaurants and parking spots fill up immediately preceding any home games. If you are not taking in the game, plan to get seated for dinner/drinks after tip off. The newly built Capitol District was developed with the idea of an entertainment area with multiple bars and restaurants surrounding a common area. Most venues will let you venture out into the plaza with an adult beverage as long as it's in a plastic cup. At one end is a giant Jumbotron screen usually showing games or other sporting events. The center of the plaza is taken up by an ice-skating rink in the weeks leading up to

Christmas. In No-Do, check out Blatt Beer and Table, in the shadow of TD Ameritrade Ballpark, for drinks and craft burgers.

48. ATTEND A LIVE PERFORMANCE

Omaha has several choices of theaters to see performances. The Rose Theater is home to the Omaha Theater Company and caters to children of all abilities. It is a very family friendly atmosphere with hands on activities prior to the show. Discounted vouchers can be purchased at HyVee grocery stores. A discounted voucher does not guarantee a seat to a specific show so make sure and call the theater to confirm that seats are available and then reserve your seats with the theater soon after purchasing your voucher. First opened as a vaudeville theater in the 1920s, The Orpheum Theater continues to host national singers, dancers, musicals, comedians and variety shows. Although it has been renovated, most of the fixtures, furniture and draperies are original from the 1920s. Tickets can be purchased through Ticket Omaha. Parking is available at meters on the street or at the OPPD Energy Plaza Garage west of the Orpheum and connected by an inclosed bridge over 16th Street. Students can register for the Student Rush program and receive discounted tickets to select shows. The Omaha Community Playhouse has been a staple of the Omaha Community since its founding in 1924. It provides a place for local actors to hone their skills on a local stage as well as in their Nebraska Touring Caravan which travels throughout the US and Canada. Tickets to performances can be purchased online or at the box office inside the theater. You can purchase ½ off tickets on the day of the show starting at noon at the box office. Bring cash or check because the box office does not accept credit/debit cards. I prefer to sit in the balcony where I always have a great view of the stage.

The Omaha Symphony performs at the Holland Performing Arts Center as well as other touring musical acts. Tickets to these shows can also be purchased through Ticket Omaha. The Holland is an easy walk from the Old Market. If you choose a Sunday performance, metered parking is free. I usually find fairly close parking on the north site of the Arts Center or there is valet parking available on the East side. The BLUEBARN Theatre has been producing plays in the Omaha area since 1989, but has recently moved to its permanent home at 1106 south 10th St. in a striking building with a rusted metal front facade. Just a short walk south of the Old Market, BLUEBARN is a non-profit professional theatre that specializes in contemporary performances. According to their website, the BLUEBARN has produced over 100 plays since their opening, while maintaining a reputation for high quality entertainment.

49. OR GO TO A MOVIE

Omaha has a large selection of movie theaters throughout the metro area. The Alamo Draft Houses and the Aksarben Theater both serve alcohol to moviegoers. The Alamo Draft House will also serve food to you at your seat. All the AMC theaters have reclining seats including foot rests. Film Streams is a nonprofit organization that describes itself as "committed to screening films based on their creative, artistic and social merits". They have 3 screens at 2 locations: Ruth Sokolof Theater at 1340 Mike Fahey Street and the Dundee Theater at 4952 Dodge Street. Here you can watch new film theatrical debuts, classic films, and Q&A with visiting filmmakers.

They also provide collaborative screenings with other community nonprofits to start discussions about important topics in Omaha.

50. VISIT A CHAPEL OR CATHEDRAL WITH BEAUTIFUL ARCHITECTURE

On a bluff overlooking I-80 and the Platte River valley near Gretna, the glass walled Holy Family Shrine was designed for travelers. This chapel is welcoming to all. It is an architectural marvel from its glass walls, red cedar columns, and water stream that runs through the chapel from the door to the altar. Outside, there is a paved path that takes you through the stations of the cross. To get to the shrine, take I-80 west towards Lincoln to the Hwy 31 Gretna exit. Head south on Hwy 31 for about 1.5 miles and then turn west (right) onto Pflug Road for about 1.5 miles. There are signs on Hwy 31 to guide you. The Cloisters on the Platte are located 3 miles south on Hwy 31 from the Holy Family Shrine. You can attend a spiritual retreat or just stop in to see the 14 sculptures on their Stations of the Cross 2500-foot-long trail. To get there, continue south on Hwy 31 to Fishery Rd, take a right and it will lead you to the Cloisters. Saint Cecilia Cathedral at 701 N 40th Street was built in 1907 in the Spanish Colonial architectural style. Along with 52 stained glass windows, it also houses a Spanish colonial art collection from Mexico, central America, and Peru. They also host an annual Flower Festival with music, art, and of course, flowers.

TOP REASONS TO BOOK THIS TRIP

You can say you've been somewhere that many of your friends have not.

Omaha has the best zoo in the world, literally!

You like food, really good food, and Omaha has a wide variety with much of thc food grown nearby!

OTHER RESOURCES:

Visitomaha.com

Trailshaveourrespect.org

Parks.cityofomaha.org

Ticketomaha.com

PACKING AND PLANNING TIPS

A Week before Leaving

- Arrange for someone to take care of pets and water plants.
- Email and Print important Documents.
- Get Visa and vaccines if needed.
- Check for travel warnings.
- Stop mail and newspaper.
- Notify Credit Card companies where you are going.
- Passports and photo identification is up to date.
- Pay bills.
- Copy important items and download travel Apps.
- Start collecting small bills for tips.
- Have post office hold mail while you are away.
- Check weather for the week.
- Car inspected, oil is changed, and tires have the correct pressure.
- Check airline luggage restrictions.
- Download Apps needed for your trip.

Right Before Leaving

- Contact bank and credit cards to tell them your location.
- Clean out refrigerator.
- Empty garbage cans.
- Lock windows.
- Make sure you have the proper identification with you.
- Bring cash for tips.
- Remember travel documents.
- Lock door behind you.
- Remember wallet.
- Unplug items in house and pack chargers.
- Change your thermostat settings.
- Charge electronics, and prepare camera memory cards.

READ OTHER GREATER THAN A TOURIST BOOKS

Greater Than a Tourist- Geneva Switzerland: 50 Travel Tips from a Local by Amalia Kartika

Greater Than a Tourist- St. Croix US Birgin Islands USA: 50 Travel Tips from a Local by Tracy Birdsall

Greater Than a Tourist- San Juan Puerto Rico: 50 Travel Tips from a Local by Melissa Tait

Greater Than a Tourist – Lake George Area New York USA: 50 Travel Tips from a Local by Janine Hirschklau

Greater Than a Tourist – Monterey California United States: 50 Travel Tips from a Local by Katie Begley

Greater Than a Tourist – Chanai Crete Greece: 50 Travel Tips from a Local by Dimitra Papagrigoraki

Greater Than a Tourist – The Garden Route Western Cape Province South Africa: 50 Travel Tips from a Local by Li-Anne McGregor van Aardt

Greater Than a Tourist – Sevilla Andalusia Spain: 50 Travel Tips from a Local by Gabi Gazon

Children's Book: *Charlie the Cavalier Travels the World* by Lisa Rusczyk Ed. D.

> TOURIST

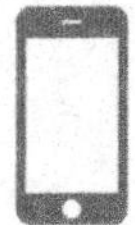

Follow us on Instagram for beautiful travel images:
http://Instagram.com/GreaterThanATourist

Follow *Greater Than a Tourist* on Amazon.

>Tourist Podcast
>T Website
>T Youtube
>T Facebook
>T Goodreads
>T Amazon
>T Mailing List
>T Pinterest
>T Instagram
>T Twitter
>T SoundCloud
>T LinkedIn
>T Map

> TOURIST

At *Greater Than a Tourist*, we love to share travel tips with you. How did we do? What guidance do you have for how we can give you better advice for your next trip? Please send your feedback to GreaterThanaTourist@gmail.com as we continue to improve the series. We appreciate your constructive feedback. Thank you.

METRIC CONVERSIONS

TEMPERATURE

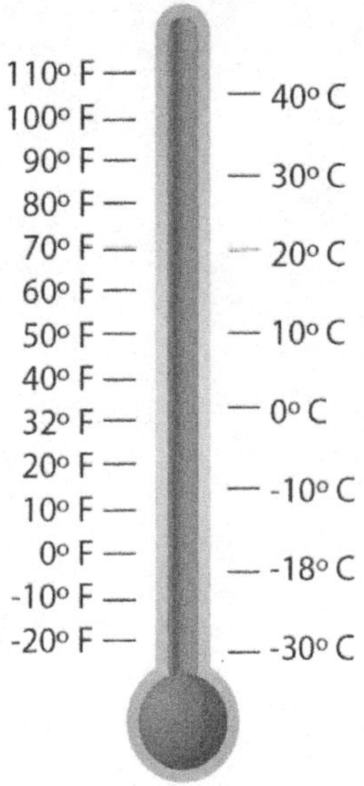

110° F —
100° F —
90° F —
80° F —
70° F —
60° F —
50° F —
40° F —
32° F —
20° F —
10° F —
0° F —
-10° F —
-20° F —

— 40° C
— 30° C
— 20° C
— 10° C
— 0° C
— -10° C
— -18° C
— -30° C

To convert F to C:

Subtract 32, and then multiply by 5/9 or .5555.

To Convert C to F:

Multiply by 1.8 and then add 32.

32F = 0C

LIQUID VOLUME

To Convert:....................Multiply by

U.S. Gallons to Liters................. 3.8

U.S. Liters to Gallons 26

Imperial Gallons to U.S. Gallons 1.2

Imperial Gallons to Liters....... 4.55

Liters to Imperial Gallons 22

1 Liter = .26 U.S. Gallon

1 U.S. Gallon = 3.8 Liters

DISTANCE

To convert ....Multiply by

Inches to Centimeters 2.54

Centimeters to Inches 39

Feet to Meters......................... .3

Meters to Feet 3.28

Yards to Meters 91

Meters to Yards 1.09

Miles to Kilometers 1.61

Kilometers to Miles............ .62

1 Mile = 1.6 km

1 km = .62 Miles

WEIGHT

1 Ounce = .28 Grams

1 Pound = .4555 Kilograms

1 Gram = .04 Ounce

1 Kilogram = 2.2 Pounds

TRAVEL QUESTIONS

- Do you bring presents home to family or friends after a vacation?
- Do you get motion sick?
- Do you have a favorite billboard?
- Do you know what to do if there is a flat tire?
- Do you like a sun roof open?
- Do you like to eat in the car?
- Do you like to wear sun glasses in the car?
- Do you like toppings on your ice cream?
- Do you use public bathrooms?
- Did you bring a cell phone and does it have power?
- Do you have a form of identification with you?
- Have you ever been pulled over by a cop?
- Have you ever given money to a stranger on a road trip?
- Have you ever taken a road trip with animals?
- Have you ever gone on a vacation alone?
- Have you ever run out of gas?

- If you could move to any place in the world, where would it be?
- If you could travel anywhere in the world, where would you travel?
- If you could travel in any vehicle, which one would it be?
- If you had three things to wish for from a magic genie, what would they be?
- If you have a driver's license, how many times did it take you to pass the test?
- What are you the most afraid of on vacation?
- What do you want to get away from the most when you are on vacation?
- What foods smell bad to you?
- What item do you bring on ever trip with you away from home?
- What makes you sleepy?
- What song would you love to hear on the radio when you're cruising on the highway?
- What travel job would you want the least?
- What will you miss most while you are away from home?
- What is something you always wanted to try?

- What is the best road side attraction that you ever saw?
- What is the farthest distance you ever biked?
- What is the farthest distance you ever walked?
- What is the weirdest thing you needed to buy while on vacation?
- What is your favorite candy?
- What is your favorite color car?
- What is your favorite family vacation?
- What is your favorite food?
- What is your favorite gas station drink or food?
- What is your favorite license plate design?
- What is your favorite restaurant?
- What is your favorite smell?
- What is your favorite song?
- What is your favorite sound that nature makes?
- What is your favorite thing to bring home from a vacation?
- What is your favorite vacation with friends?
- What is your favorite way to relax?
- Where is the farthest place you ever traveled in a car?

- Where is the farthest place you ever went North, South, East and West?
- Where is your favorite place in the world?
- Who is your favorite singer?
- Who taught you how to drive?
- Who will you miss the most while you are away?
- Who if the first person you will contact when you get to your destination?
- Who brought you on your first vacation?
- Who likes to travel the most in your life?
- Would you rather be hot or cold?
- Would you rather drive above, below, or at the speed limited?
- Would you rather drive on a highway or a back road?
- Would you rather go on a train or a boat?
- Would you rather go to the beach or the woods?

TRAVEL BUCKET LIST

1.

2.

3.

4.

5.

6.

7.

8.

9.

10.

NOTES

Made in the USA
Monee, IL
25 March 2025

14613216R00059